AF342135

**Pictures from
Bhagavad-gītā As It Is**
And Other Poems

OTHER BOOKS BY
SATSVARŪPA DĀSA GOSWAMI

Readings in Vedic Literature
A Handbook for Kṛṣṇa Consciousness
He Lives Forever
Śrīla Prabhupāda-līlāmṛta (Vols. 1–6)
The Twenty-six Qualities of a Devotee/
Vaiṣṇava Behavior
Letters from Śrīla Prabhupāda (Vol. 1)
Japa Reform Notebook
The Voices of Surrender and Other Poems
Remembering Śrīla Prabhupāda (Vols. 1–6)
Life With the Perfect Master
In Praise of the Mahājanas and Other Poems
Prabhupāda Nectar (Vols. 1–5)
Living With the Scriptures (Vol. 1)
Reading Reform
The Worshipable Deity and Other Poems
Under the Banyan Tree
Journal and Poems (Books 1–3)
Guru Reform Notebook
Prabhupāda-līlā
Dust of Vrindaban
Lessons From the Road

Pictures from Bhagavad-gītā As It Is
And Other Poems

Satsvarūpa dāsa Goswami

The
Gītā-nāgārī Press
Virginia Beach, VA

Readers interested in the subject matter of this book are invited by the Gītā-nāgarī Press to correspond with its Secretary.

*Gītā-nāgarī Press
138 South Rosemont Road #217
Virginia Beach, VA 23452*

*Printed in the United States of America
Limited edition: 2,000 copies*

Library of Congress Cataloging in Publication Data
Gosvāmī, Satsvarūpa Dāsa, 1939–
Pictures from Bhagavad-gītā As It Is and Other Poems.
   1. Vaiṣṇava poetry, American. I. Title.
PS3557.0793P5   1987   811'.54   87-11960
ISBN 0-911233-41-5

Contents

I

Pictures From Bhagavad-gītā As It Is[*]

[*]The poems are numbered to correspond with the illustrations as they are numbered in the Complete Revised and Enlarged Edition of the Bhagavad-gītā As It Is, © 1983 the Bhaktivedanta Book Trust.

Pictures From *Bhagavad-gītā As It Is*
His Divine Grace

Starting with His Divine Grace,
A. C. Bhaktivedanta Swami Prabhupāda,
sitting under a picture of Govinda.
Prabhupāda's knee is bare,
like Govinda's,
both persons wear flower garlands,
Kṛṣṇa the Lord, speaker of the *Gītā,*
and Prabhupāda, "the greatest exponent
of Kṛṣṇa consciousness in the Western world."

The photo was taken at Laguna Beach,
where he stayed for only one day.
The Preface written in Australia,
the purports written mostly in New York,
and now he has gone back to Govinda,
leaving us *Bhagavad-gītā As It Is.*

Dear Prabhupāda, let us read His book,
with your exact translations,
and your personal ecstasies.
This is the way to Gopāla Kṛṣṇa:
The only way to freedom
from birth and death.

1

For blind Dhṛtarāṣṭra,
Sañjaya, with mystic vision,
sees and retells
what's happening on the battlefield.

He points to his heart
and we also can see
Kṛṣṇa driving the horses,
Arjuna on the chariot.
But how can he see from so far away?
And why is the other man blind?

The *Gītā* is like that—
some see it clearly, by the grace of Vyāsa,

and some are so blind
they think of Kurukṣetra
as a symbol for the body;
when Sañjaya points out warriors
they think he means the senses.

The blind king frets
in fearful opposition:
"Will the influence
of the holy place defeat me?
Can I actually hope to win
with Kṛṣṇa against me?"
To be in his shoes,
even while grasping the royal scepter,
who could be peaceful?

2

Enemies of Kṛṣṇa,
Duryodhana and Droṇa.
Both are strong men,
heavy swords,
and they fight with honor.

Droṇa, you have erred,
said Duryodhana—you should not
have taught secrets
to the son of Drupada
who opposes us today.
So don't make more mistakes,
like your biggest blunder—
teaching Arjuna,
and don't be soft with the Pāṇḍavas.

Droṇācārya heard with tolerance.
He won't be soft,
but neither does he regret—
teaching those who now oppose him.
Life is meant for fighting—
for teaching fighting
& for dying in fighting—
and this is the place for it,

2

against Lord Kṛṣṇa
at Kurukṣetra.

3

These are windows
to the spiritual world,
if you have transcendental eyes.
But if you see mundane,
it's just lumps and forms,
not as real as what is happening
in your room.

How to bring it close?
Read the *Gītā*
and think in terms of *bhakti*.

The sounds of the conches of the Pāṇḍavas
shattered the hearts
of the sons of Dhṛtarāṣṭra.

Kṛṣṇa and Arjuna stand
with mighty arms upraised,
conch-horns to their lips,
under the yellow, war-cloud sky.

The golden-wheeled chariot,
the arrow-filled quiver,
his Gāṇḍīva bow,
their armor pieces—
when seen with devotion,
are enough
to bring a man back to Godhead.

4

It is an immense plain,
imminent war.
On the field of Kurukṣetra
the soldiers have to fight to death.

Śrī Kṛṣṇa's whip is raised,
as He looks back to His friend.

Arjuna's arm is raised,
ordering Acyuta:

O infallible one,
please draw my chariot
between the two armies.
Let me see who has come here to fight.

5

Great sages pray:
"Lord Kṛṣṇa was going to the battlefield
not to fight but to grace all the devotees
with His transcendental presence."

Now the Lord takes His place
as spiritual master;
His hand is raised in the *jñāna-mudra*
and with His reddish palm He blesses us.

The expert warrior sits,
limp right hand on his knee,
and looks up bewildered:
"How can I kill them?
Kṛṣṇa, tell me what to do."

The Lord wastes no time,
in offering benediction
and gentle reprimand.

Now *Bhagavad-gītā* will begin:
As Lord Kṛṣṇa speaks
even the armies hold off,
and the demigods gather in the sky
to see the radiant form,
of Śrī Kṛṣṇa dressed in gold—
He has come to teach us all.

6

The victim of car-accident
couldn't die at home,
but his wife and children are on hand,

4

and that makes it worse.
Everyone is crying and thinking,
"At least it didn't happen to me."
It's not funny, but neither is it sad,
if at that time you have the presence of mind:
I am not this body,
I am spirit soul.

The sage looks on;
but he is not crying
because he understands
no one is dying.
He alone sees the spirit soul,
and the Lord in the heart.

7

This is a picture of a man running.
It is one continuous image,
but at each step he is growing older,
although you cannot see it
unless you watch a long time.
He knows he is growing tired,
but he doesn't think he will die.
Gradually his steps falter,
and he talks about it with his wife.
"I am getting older."
He laughs about it,
"Some day I will die."
He slows down,
but he keeps moving forward
in darkness.
And he—
let us not look.

8

This is the "Changing Bodies" display,
something instructive about mankind.
Let's watch it.
Can you see down there on the left?
It's a human skull!
Beside it is an embryo—

5

it's definitely symbolic, because
you would never find an embryo
lying on the ground
unless maybe some clinic threw it out.

See above the embryo?
There is a chubby baby
lying in clover.
Now see a continuous stream
of light,
the soul is transferring
from the baby on his back
to a baby that crawls,
then a baby that walks,
playing with a hoop,
then a stick (his legs are getting stronger),
now he's an athlete,
then an almost grown-up schoolboy,
and there in the center of the page—
    the perfection!
A broad-chested man with a red toga . . .

The rest is not so interesting,
but I get the idea, one grows older,
but does it mean
we have to go exactly like that,
with a white beard?
Of course, when you get *that* old,
then you are talking of death . . .

In the distance
see the light-stream is carrying off the spark,
to another young body, and far off,
another growing older, a death again,
then you can't see it any more;
there is just a shining sun
over a dark plain, and nothing else;
it is all over.

It's interesting, but what
does it have to do with me?

9

Because He is the ideal preacher
of Kṛṣṇa's message in this age,
the picture of Lord Caitanya
belongs in *Bhagavad-gītā*.
"Be thou happy by this *yajña*.
Its performance will bestow
everything upon you
for living happily
and achieving liberation."

Everyone may hear
and join the chanting
led by Lord Kṛṣṇa
in His most merciful form.

His feet on the road,
make bright-day shadows.
The earth and grass,
palm trees and *pārijātas*,
all join with Him
in resounding *kīrtana*.

10

Thousands of years ago,
in bodies that do not burn,
Lord Kṛṣṇa first taught
the *Gītā* to the sun-god,
four-armed, gold-helmeted Vivasvān.
Vivasvān taught the *yoga*
to the father of mankind
and Manu instructed it to Ikṣvāku.

When I first heard this from Śrīla Prabhupāda
I thought, "This link is wonderful—
going back millions of years
to ancient, mystical India
like a ray of light in a short time
and the whole length alive
so when the teacher of today speaks
you can touch eternity,

provided he speaks
what Kṛṣṇa said."

Arjuna wondered,
How could my friend
speak so long ago
to a god in the sun?
He forgot
the many lives he had passed,
but Kṛṣṇa remembered them.

Sañjaya sees all
by his mystic vision,
and so may we today
by following *paramparā*.

11

When there is a decline in religion
and a rise in irreligion,
the Lord appears
in many transcendental forms:
the original is Kṛṣṇa.

The bluish boy,
His toe in a stream,
plays on His flute,
He who is the source of everything;
and the sun and moon move in fear of Him.

"But why not Lord Buddha? What about Christ?
Who is the Fish?
Who is this Boar?
What is this Lion-Man,
and why does He kill?
Aren't these stories,
like the epic of Rāma?"

With his eyes he cannot see,
the science of God,
but as he hears
from *Bhagavad-gītā*

8

a sincere soul
will gradually see
God in His tortoise pastime,
the Earth-uplifting Boar,
the Lion-Man Protector:
the Universal Form who pierces His foot
through the shell of the universe,
the Supreme Rāma and His consort Sītā,
Buddha, Christ, Mahomet,
the avenging Prince on a white horse,
and Śrī Kṛṣṇa, the Source,
in the groves of Vṛndāvana.

12

At Ramaṇa-reti
by the river Yamunā
there is a back road
where trees and people and animals
meet at a junction.
But there is no confrontation
if you can see
the soul and Supersoul.

I want to go there
and see the cow and dog
and the dog-eater and the *brāhmaṇa*
and see the soul in each,
and see the Supersoul in each.

I'll not be afraid of the elephant,
I will not curse the dog-eater
or torture the dog,
and the *brāhmaṇa* I will respect
because Lord Viṣṇu is in his heart.

His youthful body glows
a beautiful blue,
His smile dries up the ocean of tears.
and His arched eyebrows
conquer the god of love.

9

Viṣṇu, Mādhava, Vāsudeva, Kṛṣṇa,
You are fully present in Your name,
but I have to give myself
starting with surrender of my tongue.
I'll chant Hare Kṛṣṇa
and bow down in Your temple.
You will accept me
as I hear the *Bhāgavatam*.

13 & 14

In a solitary place he has to go
without material desire,
and the result of renunciation
is that Viṣṇu is pleased
and reveals Himself
in the heart of the *yogī*.

But it is not so easy.
He will have to practice
for hundreds of years
while vines grow up his forearms
and his nails and hair grow astonishingly long.
His eyes roll upwards,
and tigers roam in the night.
But if he dies during the dark moon
then his soul will come back again
to the worlds of death.

No one knows
this form of Viṣṇu
except His devotee.

16

His arms and head are blue,
his chest is fire-red,
the water gushing is his hips,
and his legs are earthen,
this man who runs
through the universe.

10

And he is afraid
as he looks back,
as he runs through the darkness.

                17
How could any person be as big
as Mahā-Viiṣṇu?
"He has to be that big
for the universe to come out
from His pores."
Things that are inconceivable
cannot be argued by logic.

Śrī Kṛṣṇa is smaller
in His original form,
yet the Big, and *everything*
emanates from Him.

Truth and beauty is Viṣṇu!
The beautiful form of a youth,
who is Supreme Godhead,
eternity, knowledge, and bliss.
With any one of His senses
He can perform all functions.
He impregnates with His eyes
and He eats by hearing prayers.

So when the universes emanate
from Viṣṇu's gigantic body
that is a small task for Him,
because His real enjoyment
is above, in Goloka
where He jauntily leans
on His cowherd staff
and calls the spotted cows.

                18
He's turning to Kṛṣṇa because his
two babies are bawling and clinging.
And he can't feed them.

His legs and head hurt,
so he calls out to God.

The businessman
is plunging into the red.
Debtors pursuing,
the law is on his case—
either jump out the window,
or pray to God for help!

The student is curious,
he reads the great books
and not just for school grades.
He thinks maybe there is one Supreme,
"And I would like to know Him."

Best of all is the sage
who understands there must be God
'tho he doesn't know Him yet.
His quest is best,
because he's ready
to surrender.

The four impious men:
one is like an ass carrying a big bag,
who thinks his duty is to toil,
but he doesn't know for whom.
The lowest of mankind has just killed his mate.
The educated fool keeps a fetus in a bottle.
And the demon shakes his fist—
he plans to rule the world.
All of them are doomed.

19

The youth is reaching for a diploma
while worshiping Sarasvatī.
A youth is pleading for the hand
of a beautiful girl
by worshiping Umā.
A sick man prays to the sun-god
while grasping the medicinal vial.

12

But even if they grant
the shining diploma,
the soft woman,
the health elixir—
death will cheat them.

Beyond all gods and death,
is Kṛṣṇa in His blissful bower
where He contemplates a *surabhi*
and waits for the return
of all souls who finish
their greedy worship
of the death-cheated gods.

20

I don't deny Kṛṣṇa
like the *mūḍhas* in the picture,
smokers and drinkers,
called *pāṣaṇḍīs* in the *Bhāgavatam*.
I can refute them and prove to them
they don't know God, or Kṛṣṇa—
He who looks like a boy
but who controls the universe.

He appears like a male youth,
and we are also in His image.
But to understand Kṛṣṇa
your heart must be pure
by service to His devotee.
They make a great mistake
who deride Him
because of His humanlike form.

Govinda, I pray
to this picture of You,
let me see past the appearance.
Everything comes from Your body alone.

21

An altar! What genius!
A festival for the senses,

13

starting with the lower step,
the golden imprints of Prabhupāda's feet.
And each *ācārya* wears a garland.
The next shelf up holds silver platters,
delectable food offered by cooks
who are not always perfect
but they are trying
to offer their devotion.

Behold Rādhā-Kṛṣṇa
within a golden throne,
surrounded by wild flowers,
wearing rose and lotus garlands.
Their gold crowns are studded
with red and blue gems,
and Their *pūjārī* in the foreground,
blissful, clean, and shaven-headed
is offering yet another flower
at Their lotus feet.

22

The young artist tried her best
with flowers of this world
and swans in water,
but Kṛṣṇa and Balarāma
are not her creations
or creations of this world.
As described in *śāstra*,
They can only be seen
with love-anointed eyes.
The cowherd boys
don't care to discourse
whether Kṛṣṇa is God
but, "Who can be the first
to touch Him!"

Doves aflutter,
He runs ahead.
Their shouts fly after Him
across the gentle river,
through flowers of ecstasy.

14

Playing on His flute,
the melody is heard
in the spiritual world.
"Kṛṣṇa! Lead on!"

23 & 24

Arjuna agreed to see
the Universal Form
because he wanted to prove
that Kṛṣṇa was no mortal being:
He is beyond the *avatāras,*
He is the source of all.

But it is not possible
to worship Viśvarūpa.
Where can you find
enough cloth to dress Him?
Or a garland big enough?
And where is the worshiper
who loves Him?

With sharp swords gigantic in size,
fire from His mouth,
the devouring giant
is Time Himself
with thousands of limbs and heads.

So what artist can paint Him?
They have tried to suggest
infinite bodies expanding in all directions,
and awe-struck Arjuna is portrayed,
looking upward with folded hands.

But we can only imagine
the shape of Viśvarūpa
shown one day to Kṛṣṇa's friend
and to others who were blessed
with divine eyes.

In response to Arjuna
the Lord at last ceased
the "godless display,"
returning to a four-armed form
and then to the form of Kṛṣṇa
standing with His friend
on the chariot of Agni.

Now there was no doubt.

25

I've seen lotus flowers
in Guyana, big pink ones
with firm whorls
like platforms one could stand on,
if you were small enough.
They grow by the roadside
and in flooded meadows.

But I have never seen
a beautiful person standing on a lotus,
or a four-armed youth
with a lotus in His hand.

Apāṇi-pādo javano grhītā:
He has no hands,
yet He accepts our offerings.
He has no eyes,
yet He sees everything.
With His spiritual legs
He can travel through space.

O Supersoul, please give me intelligence
to worship You and chant Your names.
You are in my heart, within each atom
and Your thinking is never distracted.
O You are the original Godhead.

I do not see
Your face, hands, and legs
but when I am raised

16

to pure devotion
then I will see
You are everywhere.

26

In this picture you can't see
what is happening in the shopping malls
no bodies on the battlefields—
can't see the ants crawling,
and you can't see into politician's chambers.
It appears to be a great sphere
with planets and oceans
but after all, it is a ball,
floating in space
under the control of the Lawmaker.

The thick cosmic egg
has a seven-layered shell,
but even as we sit enchained
within the prison-body,
Kṛṣṇa has penetrated
into our hearts.

And He is out there
beyond the walls of the world
in the free-spirit zone
in the ever-varied
boundless forest of Vṛndāvana.

See if you can
flowering desire trees,
walkways of gems,
devotees who love Him,
in triumph of servitude.
Look within the lotus whorl:
He is the main attraction.

The love She shares
with Kṛṣṇa
She offers to everyone.
With flower garlands,

17

and dancing to His flute,
we can join the *gopīs*
within the white lotus.
All we need
is to heed His call,
leaving the cosmic orbit
through this window.

27 & 28
From lust this woman
gets the body of a tree.
From sloth this woman
gets the body of a bear.
From eating meat
he becomes a tiger.
And the garbage-belly man
becomes a hog.

You want to be naked?
Nature gives a body
to do it even better—
a body that is naked always.
But because you abused
the human form of life
your nakedness is out in the cold.

Teeth and jaws of a tiger
do much better in tearing flesh
but you'll have to be a stalker—
catch prey only once a month.

As you drooled in lobster pus,
you may do it better
rolling in stool as a pig.

You get what you are
and all that you did.

The painting is to shock them.
Half a face turns hairy
like a Hollywood wolfman—

smooth-skin to bear-skin
pearly teeth to fangs.
If it seems to you a myth,
then what is your logic?
Can you get away with murder?
"Don't think deeds are *karma*-free;
every seed bears fruit in time."

Sometimes you can see it—
by doglike action
a man transforms.
The faces of slaughter cows
make one wonder what they did.
Why risk so many births
on the wheel of *saṁsāra*?
Don't think you're unique
to go unscathed.

You get what you are
and all that you did.

29

Purple Lust,
Bluish Anger with orange hair,
their ropes around his neck,
lead the prisoner down
until he doesn't need their pull
as he plummets forward
grasping for jewels
or is he grasping for her body
as he falls into the pit?

Going Down:
Plunging into red
with long hair and mustache—
he looks like an old friend of mine.

The largest figure
is a woman with mascara.
Why would he want those jewels?

19

A man named Jīva
plunges to hell.

Going Up:
Leaving long hairs,
with a springy step.

He approaches *guru*—
the way
to Rādhā-Kṛṣṇa.

                    30
Professor O'Reilly suggested
that ISKCON leaders should
ban the word *demon.*
'Tho I suppose he might allow
for someone as ancient
and evil as Rāvaṇa
especially if he's taken as a myth.

But Prabhupāda said *demon,*
from the Sanskrit *asura*—
and *rascal* is for *mūḍhāḥ.*
So call a spade a spade.
It's Kṛṣṇa who condemns them.

The demons
are the enemies of the world.
They *plan* for mass destruction.
Not incidentally,
but from godless science,
from mass *karma*
the nuclear cloud erupts
and everyone's within it.

Mass culture exploding into ash:
the grimacing beer-drinker,
wine girl in blue,
pigs under the table pulling the tablecloth,
humans eating cow flesh,
businessmen ogling

a naked dancer on the table,
blood-stained cow butcher,
doctor throwing the fetus in the trash,
unmarried groin to groin,
roulette, homosex, money-spent—
all within the golden fireball
sucked up with nature's forests—
our man-made destruction.

The myth of the innocent
is exposed in a red sky.
Tell us Professor O'Reilly,
what name do you have for these men?

II

Haiku

Ant on rotting stump,
as you crawl into your hole,
hear the holy name.

Bug-chewed rose bush,
give just one bloom,
and I'll offer it to Kṛṣṇa.

Reposing on the desk
they invite me once again:
my red *japa* beads.

A brown toad hops
across the brown path.
He's no big thing. Me too.

Cold rain:
at dawn a silver squirrel
cries from a branch.

Waking in the cold:
picking velvet clothes
for the Deity.

Lying in bed at dusk,
watching a few snowflakes—
the ox-cart creaks by.

Clouded dawn,
no sun or moon,
but hearing Him.

The four-day rain stops:*
children bow down
in the puddle.

--------- ◆◆◆ ---------

A rose with drops of dew:
the atheists admire
no mention of God.

--------- ◆◆◆ ---------

Rippling soft breezes from his hand,
last item of worship:
the peacock fan.

--------- ◆◆◆ ---------

A single light
cuts sickroom gloom
revealing my Lord Jagannātha.

--------- ◆◆◆ ---------

Crickets and a star.
Here also
Hare Kṛṣṇa *mantra*.

Prabhupāda

Bringing down his cane,
on Darwin's theory.

*Published in *Windchimes* magazine.

In his hand
proof of God:
a rose.

Mandir Sequence

Rock song touches
in the lead singer's *kīrtana:*
dancing in circles.

Carrying his son
in a laundry basket,
a *gṛhastha.*

While their *guru* watches
from a window—
brahmacārīs at basketball.

Willow tree now
this rainy day,
and dreams of a future temple.

Sunday Feast Sequence

During the lecture,
a guest's Irish setter
sits tied to a post.

In the crowd
a missing devotee:
shock of his black hair.

Twilight—
Hindu boys play football
on the temple lawn.

At the book table:
Datta dāsa in ecstasy—
"This is Volume Two!"

Country Ratha-Yātrā Sequence

Country Ratha-yātrā:
widening His roadway—
the sound of the scythe.

Country Ratha-yātrā:
reading my lecture
while the ducks swim by.

Country Ratha-yātrā:
along His roadway
cardinal on a fence.

Gaura-Pūrṇimā Sequence*

"Gaura-pūrṇimā is the appearance day of Lord Caitanya, an incarnation of Kṛṣṇa who taught *bhakti-yoga* in sixteenth-century India."

Sparrows
hear the chanting
as they fly from spire to spire.

Holiest day of the year—
one side of their hats turned up,
policemen move the crowds.

Walking on the road,
pilgrims in white
in the sunlight.

* Published in *Modern Haiku* magazine.

The shape of a lotus—
ironwrought window grill
frames the sky of Māyāpur.

*Year-End Sequence**

From within the body
I watch gray clouds
move through silver sky.

Nap after lunch
then back to the sled—
man and oxen.

My front tooth falls out,
a heifer is born—
last day of the year.

When guns fire at midnight
I answer from my bed,
Hare Kṛṣṇa!

* Published in *Windchimes* magazine.

III

Changing Windows

1
Delhi Airport, November 16, 1987

From here I see
all cars hitting the same bump,
but in India
every day is sunny.

I remember Vṛndāvana—
Nārāyaṇa Mahārāja's room,
how it was simple.
I would like to be a *sādhu*.
That feeling,
entering the Yamunā,
reading *Śrīmad-Bhāgavatam*,
accepting my Godbrothers
as my guides.

2
Delhi to Dublin

A 9-hour jet window
over Afghanistan, Russia,
Czechoslovakia.
All I saw below
was snow with veins,
while a man in the plane cabin snored.

Vṛndāvana memories
are fading like flowers
in a silver box.
At the baggage claim, an Irishman
in a "San Francisco" sweatshirt, said:
"Spend a few days on the streets of Dublin,
it will make a man of yuh!"

We went out in the rain to "Eason's"
looking for Irish poets and diaries,

downtown Dublin like a movie
of a cold gray city.

Stopping at "Veritas"
at the rack marked "Saints,"
I'm glad I didn't buy any
but came back quickly
to this desk facing the night.

Why should I stray away
even for an hour?
Unless I am absorbed
in *Śrīmad-Bhāgavatam*
how can I impart it?
And how can I make up
for my mistake
of imitating Prabhupāda?

3

This Baltimore window
is covered with frost
and the inscape is reformation.

Bhāgavatam is also a window—
Nārada reprimanding Vyāsa:
"Your literatures are verily condemned."
Vyāsa is glad to hear it
from his Guru Mahārāja.

My vision is frosted
by chilling *aparādhas*—
at least I know it now.
Warming up.

4
Gītā-nāgarī
I

There is seal-tight plastic
over the panes.
So you can't see
small birds clearly,
but when squirrels
jump through the air,
I see it.

& I see an orange-capped hunter,
with his rifle slung in left arm,
pacing for deer flesh,
and now he is gone.

This subtle mind-stuff!
You can't see it jump,
it doesn't have a color,
it's not reflected in the water,
but it seems more real
than the five great elements.
When I go out to walk,
it goes with me,
struggling through the mud.

II

Soon this won't be my cabin.
I will pass by and say, "Remember?"
(And then I will be gone,
and the house will change,
and the hill will die
in ten thousand years.)

Of the books I have written here,
Prabhupāda-līlāmṛta will last awhile.
When I was writing of his life
each evening seemed miraculous

as the tale unfolded—
Prabhupāda spurned by a Godbrother,
going on alone to edit BTG,
he had very little money, living in Vṛndāvana . . .
my notes came together
in this room facing the window.

III

The flowing creek is drab green,
the bankside trees are upside down,
remember and farewell.

Looking out from here
you visualized Śrī Kṛṣṇa
in a poem called "Dawn in Layers."

Twelve panes in the grid,
the squirrel's playground,
and a crude plank bench.

One day in each year hundreds come from NYC;
they wander by my window while I duck.
Once while looking out,
a woman and her lawyer rushed into view.
Searching the farm for a runaway child,
they looked at me accusingly—
was I hiding him under the desk?

And from here,
I have waited for rarities—deer, fox,
and a glimpse of their link to the Lord.

IV

In this cabin,
convalescing for a year—

Silent backyard *mantras*
dragonflies in tiger lilies
cobwebs on my bike.
"But what if I get sick again?
Where will I go to bed?"

Over the front door
the wrens keep building nests.
When my friends visit they laugh,
"It's like a hermitage!"
Canoe out the back door.

Built as a hunting cabin,
later, taken by Vāmana dāsa, his wife,
three children, and fourteen Kṛṣṇa Deities.
Now my scene—a home *sannyāsī*
with many boxloads of books,
two bathrobes,
6 sets of long underwear,
five pairs of shoes—
I'm moving out.
Don't know who is next.

V

Across this desk came the weekly editions of
U.S. News and World Report. (I used to get the *New York Times*
during the summer when Ted Kennedy and whats-
his-name were fighting for Democratic nomination.)
Now Reagan is in trouble.
Who would have thought?
The times are changing.

VI

It is sweet to close the curtains at night,
and to open them at dawn.

Goodbye, desk and lamp,
goodbye wood stove,
> pond and waterfalls,
> acorns on the roof,
> wind-chimes,
> bench under the pine tree,
> outhouse, woodchuck,
> possum,
> the damp smell,
> special picture of Lord Caitanya,
> diorama of Kṛṣṇa-Balarāma,
> file cabinets and cold floor.

VII

Since I have been here,
the trees have grown taller,
I've seen Gītā-nāgarī babies grow,
the pine boards in the cabin are darker,
and some disciples have gone away, like
my Vaiṣṇava dāsa, Lalitā, Paramahaṁsa.

VIII

Was my long poem to Rādhā-Dāmodara
another pretense?
No!
But I must serve Him in separation
like many other *bhaktas*
who adore His spritely form.
His picture in my mind,
I'll chant and hear His glories.

IV

ISKCON Pictures

Temple Opening in Ireland

Mahārāja Pṛthu leveled the land,
brought 250 truckloads of gravel,
a gold and silver altar
for Śrī Govinda
and Our Lady of Inis Rath.

While pouring milk, yogurt, *ghee*
honey and fresh juices,
we tasted the pleasure of bathing Them.

Splashing clear water
over Rādhārāṇī's shoulder
I suddenly recalled that Prabhupāda said,
"Just pour it on Her *head*!"

For Irish understanding:
"Don't you worship your icons
of Jesus, Mary, and the saints?"

According to *śāstra*
a devotee meditates
as the Supersoul expands
into the marble form.
My hand on His chest
is for me to remember:
I am His servant's servant.

When we removed the cotton from their eyes,
Rādhā and Kṛṣṇa looked out
to 300 Hindus from Belfast,
and 500 Dubliners,
while 100 Lough Erne farmers
gazed on in admiration.

On Landing in Trinidad

Our family of Deities,
headed by Śrīla Prabhupāda
appears on a table
in the Trinidad hotel.
He allows us
to bathe Them in cool water.

And by six a.m. tomorrow,
with government permission,
we head for Guyana,
to speak *bhāgavat-dharma*.

Kīrtana in Guyana, Sunday Afternoon

As you look upon the forms
of Lord Caitanya and Nityānanda—
you forget what's in your head
(Gaura's shirt is pink,
Nitāi's is grape, like purple).
And They seem to lift
the whole world
with Their upraised arms.
For Them it is no effort;
it's Their mercy.
And we dance until the floorboards bounce.

White lotuses in a vase,
Prabhupāda bare-armed,
Nṛsiṁhadeva with Lakṣmī's
small hand around His waist.
Keep looking, I tell myself,
from Deity to Deity
wherever you go
then there's a good chance
you will be near
the Kṛṣṇa Deity
at the time of death.
You will be chanting then.
At least that is my prayer—
to be near Them at the end.

The Sunday crowd is murmuring,
honoring *prasādam*
while the daylight fades on coconut trees,
and last flights of the banana quits,
just before mosquito time.
Lord in the heart,
please allow me
to sing a Kṛṣṇa conscious song
in the family of devotees.

        —Western Demerara, August 10, 1986

Just be Sure to Steer to Kṛṣṇa

If I want to write of a devotee's life,
why not write of a great one?
So I wrote of Prabhupāda
and I continue to do so,
but until I know his ongoing *līlā*
whatever I have already said
is mostly all I know, for now.

I can write of the *mahājanas*,
but I don't know much about them,
except what I've already said.
I also praise my brothers
but in that I'm also faulty.
So I write of myself.

One soul
represents the universe of souls.
As a grain of cooked rice
gives the taste of the whole,
one soul honestly revealed
gives hope, by sharing.

One soul's illusion
is like the bondage of all.
And one soul's getting free holds the key.

As a Godbrother wrote to me,
"Give me suggestions
how to act as *guru*,
there is no point in me committing
the same mistakes as you."

Just be sure to steer to Kṛṣṇa,
describe the link with Him
as service to His pure devotee.

Late Flight

The plane is rolling over a white highway of clouds, and a large, late moon is guiding the way. I hear Śrīla Prabhupāda singing with the devotees Hare Kṛṣṇa *mantra* from December 1966.

> Egg-shaped moon,
> you are also
> part of Hare Kṛṣṇa.
>
> All this jet travel
> is merely creeping
> along the surface
> of a tiny planet
> within the smallest universe.
>
> O Indweller in all things,
> please keep us close to You.
> As we travel
> let us act on Your behalf,
> and please protect us
> from forgetfulness of You—
> O Supreme Personality of Godhead.

After Reading "The Mountain Poems"
of Stonehouse (Shih-wu)

I am depending on another
for my income,
not like a hermit on a mountain,
though I admire that
romance of a recluse with the Absolute—
just eating wild plants
patched robe, white hairs,
talk of everyday things,
denouncing the world of *karma*.
But it's not so wonderful
when they spout Zen-nothings,
even then I like them,
hoary, alone with Nature,
well-spoken about freedom.

But what do they know?
I am made by Prabhupāda
for carrying the burden
of loving service—
help the people of the world,
coach younger brothers,
stay pure in the midst of Kali-yuga.

I can't talk of clouds only
and of renouncing begging and
being very calm and still and poor,
& because I've got a luminous wristwatch
doesn't mean a thing is bad,
so long as we use it in His service.
The Way—that's Kṛṣṇa;
and Nothing doesn't exist.
It's Kṛṣṇa alone who
controls all monks
and worldly fools,
and He is the Lord.
I'm glad I'm a servant
of a *bhakta*.

First Night in Vṛndāvana

Why couldn't you sleep?
Bugs were biting me,
and I thought of my neighbors:
Tārkṣya's on the left,
Hayagrīva's on the right.
Did I dream of Rāmānuja?
I thought of the morning.

As hours passed slowly,
I sat up and listened
to crickets in Vṛndāvana.
I thought of writing a book:
"Arguments Against Buddhism."
But it will take a long time
for me to comprehend.

I thought about ISKCON
and its divergent ways,
until I concluded,
"Kṛṣṇa is in charge."
I decided not to join
the snackbar *prajalpa*.
Then I turned on the light.

Hearing Śukadeva En Route

In the empty plane,
stopped in Pittsburg,
Bala is readying the apples,
while imitation soul music
pours down on us
from the cool air vents
where the oxygen masks are stored.
It's a male-female duet,
"Lonely is the night
when I'm not with you."
But I don't buy it.
Heading for Dallas,
thinking of my Godbrothers;
eager for their reprimand.

The plane fills with Musac,
so I'd better chant and read
how Śuka spoke for seven days
the essence of the *Vedas*
for those who are about to die.

Ārati

Offering the *ghee* flame
to Śrīla Prabhupāda
wrapped in his *cādar*,
this down-to-earth *pūjā*
of sublime feeling
for the worshipable deity.

Waving the handkerchief,
and gazing at the Lord's feet,
looking at the weapons of Nṛsiṁhādeva,
meditating on the form
of Bhaktisiddhānta Sarasvatī,
circling the conch,
suddenly I notice
the way Rādhā holds onto Kṛṣṇa,
and the smile of Jagannātha:
I enter Their shelter.

But I have to leave
this quiet meditation
to enter in exchange
with my Godbrothers.
We are all worshipers of Gaura-Nitāi.
That is why we come together,
even though we differ
on some essential points.

To Godbrothers

I sat on a throne above your heads
as you sat on the floor.
My lectures were not superior to yours
but we pretended
that I was supreme, "almost
as good as Prabhupāda."
Now I'm stepping down
to be what I am,
a fool before our Guru Mahārāja.

I should not have ascended above you,
even though you offered it to me.
And you said, "Here are your disciples,"
although it was you
who brought them to surrender.
I blessed them and gave them
the *mahā-mantra* and a spiritual name,
but I never told them,
"He is your *śikṣā-guru*."

You know all this and you are
willing to forgive me
but the wrong will linger.
Please let me offer
my repeated apologies;
please teach me
how to honor
my Godbrothers.

Another Day, A Glance From Him

I heard a friend wants to resign—
(I didn't tell him
the same thing's on my mind).
A day of headaches off and on,
and I recorded my pro and con.

Tomorrow, when I speak with disciples
why don't I just admit
I made a real mistake
and let them think as they like?
Because I am their teacher,
I'll ask them to forgive me.

That's for tomorrow,
but tonight I just caught
a smiling glance from Prabhupāda
while sitting under his photo
as I read *Bhagavad-gītā As It Is.*
He stands in the woods,
daṇḍa in his left hand,
his right hand fingering beads.

Pūrṇimā

In the East
a full moon
emerges through clouds,
dropping a column of gold
onto the creek.

In the West,
pink clouds.

But all nature is
just a hometown mellow
compared to Śrī Kṛṣṇa.

As the full moon emerges,
I'm chanting His names.

Prabhupāda Mūrti

Affection for you,
Prabhupāda *mūrti*,
rose up recently,
when I was ill,
maybe I was afraid,
I can't remember,
was I feeling alone?

To pick you up,
place you in bed,
awaken you,
to bathe your tan, effulgent form,
all these acts become dear to me again.
You are accompanying me
through the last days of my life.

But I have to *act* on your behalf.
I need more
than a dream,
or a quote in my ear,
I need the gumption,
to surrender to your Movement.
I need faith as strong as śāstric injunction
to know that what I am doing is right.
Please grant me conviction.

V

*Discovered Poems of
Śrīla Prabhupāda Talking*

Introduction

Modern poets have found almost-complete poems in unlikely
places, such as newspaper articles, a child's talking, a piece of
prose by a serious writer, or the speaking of an exceptional person.
For example, in 1935, W. B. Yeats, while editing the *Oxford Book of
Modern Verse*, reprinted Pater's paragraph on Mona Lisa, rearrang-
ing it to look like *vers libre*. In a recent book, the American poet
Jane Cooper, describes her poem *Inheritances* as "almost verbatim
from Herter Norton's translation of Rilke's *The Notebooks of Malte
Laurids Brigge*." And Joel Openheimer, in *Poetry, the Ecology of the
Soul*, describes his "found" poem, *At Fifty*, as follows: "It is word
for word (from a newspaper clipping); with a possible alteration
in some of the punctuation where it may have been broken into
separate sentences while I've made it a list. But I have not changed
any words, any meanings."

In such poems, the poet acts mostly as an editor, discovering
art in an unusual context. By sensitively placing his discovery in
the format of a poem he gives us—if he is successful—a fresh and
valid expression. This is not the same thing as "versifying," which
implies a change in words and meter, and where the new work
often becomes something entirely different from the original inspi-
ration.

Devotees who have regularly listened to Prabhupāda's
speeches have often remarked that Prabhupāda is a wonderful
speaker. Although he always repeats what he has heard from pre-
vious *ācāryas*, his expressions are original and poetic. When we
tune into Prabhupāda's speech and when we take excerpts from
it, as I have often done, we find complete poetic statements. The
poems that I have "discovered" here are left almost just as he spoke
them. In some cases I have skipped from one part of his lecture to
another and brought the sentences together without using the el-
lipsis points. Occasionally I have changed a word. But this is
Prabhupāda almost verbatim, in free-verse form. Although the
method of discovery may seem easy enough, I went through many
lectures, and selected only what I felt was the most striking and
presentable. I hope that it will be pleasing to his followers.

God is God
Śrīmad Bhāgavatam (7.9.12) Montreal, August 1968

God is God, always God!
Just like Kṛṣṇa,
in the womb of His mother, He's God,
in the lap of His mother, He's God,
while He's playing with His boyfriends
as cowherd boy, He's God,
while He's dancing with His girlfriends,
He's God,
while He's fighting in Kurukṣetra,
He's God,
while He's married, He's God,
while He's speaking, He's God,
that is God.

He's the origin of Brahmā,
He's the fountainhead of Śiva,
He's the fountainhead of Viṣṇu,
therefore He's the origin.

So our prayer should be
to the Supreme Person,
"Govindam ādi-puruṣaṁ
tam ahaṁ bhajāmi."

60

Sannyāsa

We are going alone.
This is retirement.
Without waiting for anyone.
Alone, simply depending on Kṛṣṇa.
This is the process of renouncement.

Not to make arrangement in the family,
"Now I am retiring.
You send me money
and I shall maintain myself."
No. No dependence,
simply depend on Kṛṣṇa.
Therefore it is said, *eka matir apa:*
actually Kṛṣṇa saves us.
So why should we depend on others?

On the Disappearance Day of
Śrīla Bhaktisiddhānta Sarasvatī Ṭhākura
December 9, 1968

By Kṛṣṇa's arrangement
we came in contact,
'tho I was born in one family,
and my Guru Mahārāja
was born somewhere else.

Who knew
that I would come
to his protection?
Who knew
that I would come to America?
Who knew
that you American boys will come to me?
These are all Kṛṣṇa's arrangements.
We cannot understand
how these things are taking place.

He Can Do Wonderful
January 5, 1973

Kṛṣṇa goes every day
to the forest of Vṛndāvana
and there some demon comes
and the cowherd boys say,
"There is Kṛṣṇa,
we don't care
for this demon."
And the demon is killed.

And they come home
and narrate the story:
"Oh, my dear mother,
Kṛṣṇa did this wonderful thing."
The mother is also
very appreciative:
"Oh, how our Kṛṣṇa is so nice.
He can do wonderful.
He must be some demigod."
Like that, gossiping.
So actually this is life,
this Vṛndāvana is actual life.

At The End of Kali-Yuga
January 5, 1973

What is this life, working so hard
day and night, discovering so many things!
Don't you know,
as soon as the water supply is stopped
everything stops?

The electricity will stop,
the electric train will stop,
the lift will stop, the light will stop.
And there will be havoc.
So this artificial life
is not actual life.

There will be a time
when for hundreds of years
there will be no rain.
You have to wait for that time.

That time is coming
at the end of Kali-yuga
when for hundreds of years
there will be no rain.
Everything on earth
will be burned into ashes.

Then the sunshine will be twelve times hotte
This is stated in the *Bhāgavatam*.
Everything will be burned into ashes.
And then there will be torrents of rain.
These descriptions are there.

Rādhārāṇī Janmā
Rādhāṣṭamī 1968

Don't take Rādhārāṇī
as an ordinary woman
like your wife or sister.
She's the pleasure potency!
And the birth of Rādhārāṇī
was not from the womb
of any human being.
She was found by Her father
in the field while he was plowing;
he saw one little, nice child
and he had no children
so he caught it
and presented to the queen:
"Oh, here we have got
a very nice child."
"How you got?"
"In the field. Just see."
Rādhārāṇī's *janmā* is like that.

Please Tell About Me
To Your Kṛṣṇa
September 5, 1973

Anyone who comes before Rādhā
to serve Kṛṣṇa,
Oh, She becomes so pleased.
She immediately recommends,
"Kṛṣṇa, Oh, here is a devotee,
he is better than Me."
This is Rādhārāṇī.

I may not be a devotee.
I may be most fallen rascal.
But if I try to reach Kṛṣṇa
through Rādhārāṇī,
then my business is successful.

We should worship Rādhārāṇī first.
You just put one flower
in the hands of Rādhārāṇī
"My mother, Jaganmātā,
if You kindly take this flower
and offer it to Kṛṣṇa."

Rādhārāṇī will say,
"Oh, you have brought a flower?"

So you should offer *puṣpāñjalī*
and pray to Rādhārāṇī,
"Kindly be merciful
and tell about me to Your Kṛṣṇa."

A Guruji God
September 5, 1973

The Māyāvādī *sannyāsīs* say,
Namo nārāyaṇa:
"Everyone has become Nārāyaṇa."

Everyone is God,
but the rascal God
is now in the hospital
under surgical operation,
a *guruji* god.

They have no shame—
"Even I am god
I cannot cure my bodily pains,
so what kind of god I am?"

They also say,
"Why you are finding out God?
Don't you see so many gods
are loitering in the street?"
So God has become a tiny thing for them.

But our God is different.
*Yas tu nārāyaṇaṁ devam
brahma-rudrādi-daivatiḥ
samatvena iva vikṣeta
sa pāṣaṇḍī bhaved dhruvam.*
Our Nārāyaṇa is exalted.
We cannot even compare Him
with Lord Brahmā and Lord Śiva,
so what to speak of these rascals.

I Had To Come Here

Come to the *guru*.
But nobody comes to the *guru*,
therefore *guru* has to come
to U.S.A. to canvass.
This is the position.

Nobody went to me in India,
but I had to come here
to canvass you.
Because it is Kali-yuga.

An intelligent man knows—
"My life is meant for spiritual realization.
I must find out a *guru*."
But nobody knows it,
so Caitanya Mahāprabhu taught preaching.
These rascals are so fallen
they will never search out *guru*,
so *guru* comes to canvass.

Kṛṣṇa Has Given
December 8, 1973

Kṛṣṇa is wonderful.
Either I talk or you talk.
Sweetmeat is sweet,
either you give or I give.

But a scientist will not
try to understand
that Kṛṣṇa has given us metal
and given us the intelligence
so that now we have prepared a nice airship.
And Kṛṣṇa has given us
the sky to fly.
Appreciate like that.
Then you are Kṛṣṇa conscious.

If there was no sky,
where would you fly?
And if there was no metal,
how could you manufacture?
If you have no intelligence,
how could you do it?
So everything is given by Kṛṣṇa,
and you are denying Him.
How fool you are, you see?

Miseries From Others
Śrīmad-Bhāgavatam (1.15.45) Los Angeles, December 23, 1973

You do not create any enemy,
but your neighbor is your enemy,
your friend will be enemy,
your brother will be enemy,
your son will be enemy—
this is *adhibautika*.

Somebody's dog,
you have seen.
One is passing on the road,
and the dog is so faithful,
he becomes your enemy,
Ruf! Ruf! Ruf!—
"Why are you passing here?"

The mosquito will be your enemy;
the bugs will be enemies;
the insects will be enemies.
You may go on killing with spray,
but so many, many enemies,
so many troubles
are being created.
Who has created them?
The Nature.

To give you disturbance.
Nature will create,
yet you are thinking,
"We are very happy;
we are very happy
in this material life."

Because irreligious,
therefore rascal.
"You mean big men,
big scientists,
big, big—still they are rascals?"
Yes.
"Why?"
Because irreligious.

They do not know what is God,
therefore they are rascal.
This is the only test.
Do you know God?
"No, sir."
Then you are rascal,
that's all.
One test is sufficient,
whether you know God.

Kṛṣṇa Has A Headache
December 26, 1972

Just like Kṛṣṇa pretended
that He was sick,
and many physicians came.
He said, "No physician can cure Me.
But if some devotee gives Me the dust
of his feet on My head,
then I can be cured."
So all devotees were asked,
and nobody—
"Oh! How can I give
my dust on the head of Kṛṣṇa?
How is it possible?"
Nobody prepared.

Then Kṛṣṇa asked:
"Go to Vṛndāvana.
Just ask the *gopīs* if they can give,
they are My best friends.
If they are prepared?
Oh, I am very much suffering from headache."

As soon as the *gopīs* were approached:
"Oh? Kṛṣṇa is sick?
They want dust of our feet?"
Immediately—"Please take."
They did not care
that, "We are going to hell,
by offering our dust of feet
on the head of Kṛṣṇa."

"Never mind.
We shall go.
Kṛṣṇa will be happy.
That's all.
Kṛṣṇa will be happy."
That is *gopī*.

Deathlessness Begins at Initiation
January 1974

Immediately from that moment,
as soon as you are initiated,
you promise the spiritual master,
"Yes, I am initiated
and I shall act like this."
And if you follow
then your death
is stopped at that point.

No more death.
Just like you sleep
and again you awake. . .
When you rise you will see,
"I am with Kṛṣṇa."

This is a fact.
But don't fall down.
Don't be childish:
"Yes, I have promised
before spiritual master,
before Kṛṣṇa,
before fire,
but that's all right—
let me break."
Don't do that.
Don't lose this opportunity!
You are now at the point of deathlessness,
but if again you connect . . ."

VI

Sing While You May in Vṛndāvana,

Parikrama Notes

When I saw that I was not able to go out walking with the other devotees on the *vraja-maṇḍala parikrama*, I decided to write of my own limited *"parikrama"* within the confines of the Krishna-Balaram *mandir*. I decided not to be disappointed but to realize that there is an infinite amount of discovery I can make within this one *mandir*, as I go through my services at Prabhupāda's *samādhi*, in the temple, during *japa*, morning class, *kīrtanas*, study and brief walks outside the temple grounds.

It is stated in the Bible (re-created by Thoreau):

> Remember the Creator in the days of thy youth, lay up a store of natural influences. Sing while you may, before the evil days come. He that hath ears, let him hear. See, hear, smell, taste etc., while the senses are fresh and pure.

In a similar way, I thought of trying to store up memories from Vṛndāvana, for that time when I may not be able to come here. The special advantage in Vṛndāvana is that everything is connected to Kṛṣṇa. The advice, "See, hear, smell, taste etc., while the senses are fresh and pure," is perfectly applied here. Although only topmost devotees like the six Gosvāmīs are able to intensely feel the presence of Kṛṣṇa, even a neophyte can make an offering to Vṛndāvana *dhāma*, in disciplic succession.

Śrīla Prabhupāda's Samādhi Mandir

1

Circumambulating the altar, I feel a benefit beyond my perception. At 4:10 A.M., suddenly the *pūjārī* opens the wooden doors, and *Prabhupāda is here.* I stand close to the *mūrti.* Now nine years and three months since November 14, 1977.

2

Sometimes you remember when Śrīla Prabhupāda was lowered into the ground. We were too ignorant to imagine how much guidance we lost. I did not carefully, devotedly follow him.

In the afternoon I saw Tosana Kṛṣṇa dāsa shouting and throwing stones—was chasing vultures from the dome—taking care of the *samādhi* even in its unfinished state.

3

Śrīla Prabhupāda's right hand index finger is slightly extended so he can hold *japa mālā* and finger the beads. The left hand rests on his thigh. During *maṅgala-ārati* a wooden mallet is placed in his right hand and the brass gong in his left, as he joins the *kīrtana.*

Prabhupāda has come to put out the blazing fire of material existence. His *mūrti* is shiny and catches light. Day by day we come closer to him. He is large enough to accommodate all of us, catching up our attention. He sits lightly and yet the figure is heavy as *guru* should be, and mystical, as a *bhakti-yogī.*

4

Śrīla Prabhupāda, it is you we have to follow. Otherwise, even if we know we are spirit soul, and we desire to go back to Godhead, it will not be acceptable to Kṛṣṇa. I pray to you, please allow me to accept what is pleasing to you, even if it is not my idea. You know my prayers about freedom from physical and managerial headaches and all that, but please don't let me go astray. Devotional service is like the razor's edge—we cannot be too timid or too bold. But we must be pleasing to you. In this short lifetime, please protect me from the mistakes of straying away from your direct service. For life's directions, and to immediately accomplish the goal of worshiping your lotus feet, we come daily to Prabhupāda's Samādhi Mandir.

5

Bhūrijana was singing
as if Prabhupāda was present
and he is—
in the Samādhi Mandir.

Krishna-Balarām Mandir Deities

1

The Deities stand before the parrots backdrop. Each parrot is in a different position, all in stages of flight. Together they seem to be spinning and cavorting in ecstasy behind Kṛṣṇa-Balarāma, Rādhā-Śyāmasundara, and Gaura-Nitāi.

2

Although they say it has changed from winter to spring, it is still cold in the morning before the sun rises. We like to see the Deities wearing artistic shawls—creamy white ones draped around the shoulders and neck of Kṛṣṇa-Balarāma, a red wool *cādar* wrapped around the body of the *lakṣmī* conch, the two *śīlas* with blankets around Their shoulders, and Lord Nṛsiṁhādeva completely wrapped around. The *pūjārī* wears no shirt at all, as he offers a flame.

3

A nice feature of these gorgeous Indian ISKCON *mandirs*, built by Śrīla Prabhupāda, is that you can view each of the three Deity altars, one at a time, while leaning on the marble rail, drinking in the beauty of Rādhā-Kṛṣṇa, Gaura-Nitāi, Prabhupāda, and Bhaktisiddhānta Sarasvatī *mūrtis*. I don't even know who I am (*ke āmi?*), yet I grow attached to These marble forms of the Absolute Truth. And I am grateful to Prabhupāda for training us to rise early and greet Them. We fix our eyes on the perfection of vision—and curse the mind for going elsewhere during His *maṅgala-ārati*.

4

Yesterday the Deities wore gold lamé outfits. These contrasted with the dark reddish-brown backdrops that outlined forms of arches and pillars. The *gopīs* and Śrīmatī Rādhārāṇī wore gathered skirts with short-sleeved blouses. The necklines and sleeves had intricate borders, and veils hung gracefully from Their heads. All the male Personalities wore tight pants, long-sleeved shirts—and capes and *cādars* flowed from Their shoulders. The gold lamé was comprised of a combination of turquoise, green, pink, coral, rustic gold, and purple sequins set in a raised floral pattern. The central floral design held creamy white pearls, and all the cloths were surrounded with *jārī*. A brilliant gold-plated staff leaned against Śyāmasundara while He played on His flute. The single peacock feather in His turban swayed in a soft breeze.

1

A devotee walks by, keys jangling on his waist. Prabhupāda had keys to his *almirā* and to different drawers and doors. The devotee who holds the keys today is a different man from the old days. But it is still Prabhupāda's room.

The room is darkened somewhat and we all chant together. One devotee looks at the covers of Prabhupāda's books. Haṁsarūpa dāsa chants his *japa* in an interior room, sitting before the small *āsana* Prabhupāda used when he took *prasādam*. Glass museum cases hold Prabhupāda's personal effects. We didn't realize when he was here, how important each moment was.

2

Sitting alert repeating the names outloud, I was as proud as a *gurukula* boy: "Do I earn a gold star for this?" Two *brahmacārīs* are drinking water without touching the cups' edge to their lips. They slosh the water inside their mouths and cheeks as if it were the best nectar. But the main action in Prabhupāda's room is *japa*— the temple president, the GBC, the temple commander, all chanting *japa*, pacing back and forth in *mantra* rhythms. Each day, devotion accumulates. Let's not act to lose it!

3

Each day I've been bowing down to Prabhupāda from a distance, on the other side of the velvet rope that separates visitors from his room. Today I went up close and bowed down flat before him. As I rose up, I first saw his feet under the low table, and then I faced him and thought, "Now say to Prabhupāda what's on your mind about your service." But I was ashamed to state my confusion. I remembered how Prabhupāda did not like rambling inquiries from a confused mind. He would cut through such talk to the heart of your *māyā*, like the time when he asked me, "What *are* you doing?" and I realized I was doing very little. This morning I decided to come back later and in his presence write him a letter.

4

As devotees arrive to Vṛndāvana *dhāma*, from Italy and Japan, some of the younger ones who never saw Prabhupāda, enter his room for the first time, in awe. Soon they too are chanting, side by side in *japa-yajña*.

It is a custom to present newly published books before Śrīla Prabhupāda in his room. Īśvara Swami from Brazil has placed Portugese translations of *Śrīmad-Bhāgavatam*, *Caitanya-caritāmṛta* volumes, and three *Śrīla Prabhupāda-līlāmṛta* volumes on Prabhupāda's desk. Devotees gather around Prabhupāda admiring the books and looking at the pictures. The excitement and pleasure of producing Śrīla Prabhupāda's books and presenting them to him—who can know this except the Prabhupādānugas? Śrīla Prabhupāda himself gave it great importance and he was pleased to see the books, and to hear how they were being distributed, therefore, we continue it, and we are also pleased.

Ramaṇa-reti

1

Usually around 5:00 P.M. we go down to Ramaṇa-reti and sit under a tree in a distant part of the field. I watch the orange sun going down through branches of a tree. While I was saying Gāyatrī *mantra* tonight, some dogs started harassing a hog. She keeps walking ahead herding her piglets in front of her. The dogs rarely make an all-out attack, and if they do it, it is not for killing. The ugly hogs, can they defend themselves if they have to? These distracting thoughts pass through my mind, as the hogs and dogs range across the dust-raising field of Ramaṇa-reti. At least our talk under the tree was transcendental, myself and two devotees.

Walking back to the temple we sometimes catch glimpses of ordinary scenes, which are somehow wonderful. An old man standing at the gate of an *āśrama*, gesturing with his hands, typical of Indians. At such moments, Bhārata-varṣa seems to display beautiful culture. Tonight we passed Dr. Kapoor who had a bright orange bead bag, chanting. Another old man had a faded white bead bag. In the neighborhood around Ramaṇa-reti you suddenly come upon persons who appear just like ISKCON devotees. I haven't noticed people quite so similar to ISKCON devotees in other parts of India. In Purī, for example, you won't find so many with bead bags or with Gauḍīya Vaiṣṇava *tilaka*. To suddenly see devotees standing outside their door looking very much a part of the same spiritual family we belong to, is always striking. A very wonderful neighborhood.

2

Where we go in Ramaṇa-reti is a large field, like a soccer field. In fact, the *gurukula* boys use it for that purpose daily. It's mostly bare, soft earth with some curling leaves on it. There are a few green bushes scattered throughout, but it has a desert look. There are some very special ancient trees, such as the *kalpa-vṛkṣa* tree which is supposed to be from Kṛṣṇa's time.

But the field is often tense with the interactions of dogs, hogs, and peacocks. The dogs are the swaggering bullies. Once in a while they chase a peacock off the ground until he flies to shelter on a high wall. Ramaṇa-reti was a delightful spot for Kṛṣṇa and the cowherd boys, but now it is the roaming ground of these beasts who share the field in an uneasy state, like neighbors from different ethnic groups.

3

The air is filled with sounds of birds. I know the gray, fluffy babblers and the parrots. Now the peacocks have full tail feathers. The males look radiant, with blue and purple necks and breasts and shining jewellike tails. Prabhupāda writes, "The same sounds and atmosphere still prevail in the area where our Krishna-Balaram temple is situated. Everyone who visits this temple is pleased to hear the chirping of the birds as described here (*kūjat-kokila-haṁsa-sārasa*)," (*Śrīmad-Bhāgavatam* 10. 13. 5, purport).

4

Today the field is just peacocks. When their brilliant colors become more radiant by the rays of the setting sun, and when they roam in twos and threes, one hopping or flying up to the high wall, one walking gracefully through the dust, one turning its neck, we are directly reminded of Śrī Kṛṣṇa in the original Vṛndāvana. A day of just peacocks in the field (along with one gray heifer) is a relief and a treat: "Look! Kṛṣṇa's peacocks!"

5

The sun is lingering later nowadays, past 4:30–5:00 o'clock. A worshiper has etched a design and surrounded it with sand walls just under the Kṛṣṇa-Balarāma tree. But there are piles of stool there also. In Vṛndāvana we encounter such things side by side. Worship goes on despite stark poverty and exposure of natural acts. In the same spot you will find worship as well as disregard of worship.

Two women carrying bundles of dry sticks twice their size, stop to rest. A few other groups of people sit talking in various parts of the field. Suddenly a herd of doomed goats comes around the corner, herded by a man who thinks he needs them for his livelihood. No one wears shoes. The scenes vary and shift at Ramaṇa-reti, but the land, trees, sky, and birds are constant.

6

Ramaṇa-reti is mostly silent except for nature's sounds, but today a *bhajana* blare suddenly erupted from a nearby loudspeaker. The same thing happened last night near the Krishna-Balaram *mandir*. But even annoying sounds in Vṛndāvana usually have some close connection to Kṛṣṇa.

Kīrtana

1

When we chant in the temple we are one family. I cry out
"Śrīla Prabhupāda *ki jaya!*"not caring what outsiders think, such
as sociology professors with their vertical and horizontal *communitas*
theories or those who would minimize the place of Prabhupāda.
If I cry out, "Śrīla Prabhupāda *ki jaya!*" it may not accomplish
everything, but it helps. And it helps to jump up and down in the
kīrtana hall, *karatālas* gripped tightly in hands, clanging rhythm,
glancing happily at other devotees and forgetting, "What's for
breakfast?" or "I am sick" or "I am not happy so don't try to make
me smile like a fool."

2

Time limit: I keep glancing at the clock because if the *kīrtana*
is too long, then the lecture will start late, and then I may be late
for breakfast, and then lunch will follow too soon. . . . In other
words, *kīrtana* in my opinion, shouldn't be very long.

Body limit: Feet hurt, and of course, any exertion may threaten
my head. Body-aches signal to the mind, "Don't get too much into
the *kīrtana*. And be careful to preserve your voice."

Mind limit: If the *kīrtana* leader tries too aggressively to involve
me, I resent it. I like to be close to them, but not too close. The
mind doesn't allow the pure self to relish the name—it rejects-and-
accepts, mulls and wishes, backwards and forwards.

3

Getting in close together, standing around the microphone,
happy in *kīrtana*. I can't describe the *inside* of *kīrtana*, I can only
submit an externalized after-the-fact report: "I took part enthusias-
tically in *kīrtana*." It is inexpressible, not because my experience of
the bliss-ocean is so deep, but because even a drop of *kīrtana-rasa*
is beyond external mind and words. While chanting and dancing
we receive *darśana* of the Deities. They also, are not external al-
though we see Them. *Internal* means "O Supreme Lord, You are
my master. I am Your servant." *Kīrtana-rasa* means everything is
all right.

4

Some senior devotees walk out if the *kīrtana* endures for more than ten minutes. Those who stay and chant, are they the simple devotees? Those who get restless and have to leave the *kīrtana* hall for business, are they the responsible men?

5

Induce the little boys to dance, push the eccentric *brahmacārī* who stands motionless as if he is in another world, and what about those staid *gṛhasthas* hanging way in the back as if *kīrtana* were for ruffians? Never mind improving the others, just surrender yourself, your feet, ankles, arms, head, heart—get in there!

86

We start on our *parikrama* led by the head-gardener, who only knows the Indian names of flowers.

Just outside the guesthouse is a row of dark pink petunias. They are trumpet-shaped, like morning glories, and light and silky. Lining the window of the guesthouse are pots of cross moss which are like tiny daisies, some with violet petals, and yellow whorls in the center. There is also a pink flower called *balkesi* which is another trumpet-like bloom, with oblong leaves. On the right hand side by the fence is a mixture of petunias in different shades of purple, red, and pink. There are also more *balkesis* and cross moss. On the left hand side in the window of Prabhupāda's house there are tiny white blossoms, called *chandi tup*, and a flower (like the red of geraniums) called *gulahar*.

Bearing to the left, and going around Prabhupāda's house, in front of his three large windows, are many marigolds (the Indian name is *jaffery*), poppies, and petunias. From here if we look to the right side on the outer wall there are more marigolds in a row of pots, many poppies, and *chandi tups*.

Walking straight ahead in the direction of Prabhupāda's Samādhi Mandir, there is a rock garden, pond, and fountain on the right and here are bright orange daisylike flowers called *kalenduli*, and a five-petaled flower called *kanphool* (ear flower) which has subtle and gorgeous mixtures of colors, from red to purple, against a white- colored petal.

In front of the temple, opposite the *samādhi* are rows of pink petunias, lilac-colored cross moss and marigolds. Pots lined up in front of the *samādhi* hold *kalendulis* and some pansies. There are also rows of flowers in front of the Prabhupāda museum, and on either side of the front temple entrance.

There are potted flowers on the main altars and we look through their branches and blossoms when recieving *darśana* of the Lord. And all these flowers are regularly picked for Deity garlands which are then distributed as *prasādam* to the devotees. Everyday I manage to get a couple of garlands which I drape around the *vyāsāsana* of my Prabhupāda *mūrti*.

Although the ISKCON property of Krishna-Balaram *mandir* is not very expansive, it is packed with *kṛṣṇa-bhakti* at every step. Circumambulating the temple on the path that goes between Prabhupāda's house and the temple, one is refreshed by the spring-blooming flowers.

Vṛndāvana Miscellany

1

The Trees

The residents of Vṛndāvana have a habit of stripping the trees of branches. I understand the poverty and the need of the residents, who need to keep warm and to cook, and who cannot simply turn on the thermostat for their central heating. Therefore, my sympathy for the tree is sentimental. Yet from the tree's point of view it is torture. But the tree is tolerant and never protests.

Now that spring has come, the residents may ease up somewhat from breaking the branches. But when the trees produce valuable leaves, the *nīm* merchants and others will strip them back to the bone. The whole process, however, is different than in the West where trees are raised as crops and then cut down. Here, humans and trees live together year after year. The tree supplies the man, although unwillingly, and the man never kills his tree-supplier.

None of this is present in the original Kṛṣṇa-loka where the *kalpa-vṛkṣa* trees give abundantly whatever anyone wants. And the *kalpa-vṛkṣas* are never diminished. Tree stripping is an example of anomalies in the *dhāma*, due to the age of Kali and the needs of the residents.

Prabhupāda has warned us not to judge the residents of Vṛndāvana. But when there were outright misbehaviors, Prabhupāda himself would tell us. He criticized imitation *bābājīs* who dress themselves with loincloths like Rūpa Gosvāmī but who act like materialists. In explaining these anomalies, Prabhupāda did not avoid the truth in the name of honoring the residents of Vṛndāvana. But as a defender of the *dhāma*, he showed us how one should behave in Kṛṣṇa's abode.

2

Chaukīdārs

In the dark of 4:00 A.M., I passed the watchman half slumbering in the chair beside his shotgun. They have given him a camouflage shirt and track shoes. He is wrapped in a blanket. As I pass we exchange, *"Haribol,"* *"Hare Kṛṣṇa."* Another *chaukīdār* is stationed by Prabhupāda's Samādhi Mandir, sitting in the dark. There could be attacks, even in Vṛndāvana and Prabhupāda therefore employed *chaukīdārs,* but he insisted that they should stay awake and ring

the bell on time. During the day, the *chaukīdārs* chat and play with
the babies.

3

Monkeys

They have a route to our roof from the tree-top of the next-door
yard. The tree is light-branched at top, but they lean with its weight
and reach out for the roof, usually three monkeys together. Once
they reach the roof they do mischief, such as going down the stairs
into the kitchen where they steal fruits and vegetables and run
away. I heard Haṁsarūpa had a BB gun to sting them. He said he
used it sparingly because people frown on it. He has successfully
chased the monkeys from Prabhupāda's *samādhi,* so he doesn't
mind much if they run instead up onto the guesthouse roof. I
conceded that we cannot get too rough with them. Prabhupāda
writes, "One may sometimes think that the monkeys in Vṛndāvana
are envious, because they cause mischief and steal food. But in
Vṛndāvana we find that the monkeys are allowed to take butter
which Kṛṣṇa Himself distributes. Kṛṣṇa personally demonstrates
that everyone has the right to live. . . . The inhabitants of
Vṛndāvana think, "Whatever is given by Kṛṣṇa, let us divide as
prasādam and eat."

89

Speaking and Hearing Lectures

1

While giving class you are forced to use your brain to praise
Kṛṣṇa and to clear off doubts.

> *Śāstra* is the mother
> and you praise her;
> *guru* is the father
> and you praise him
> with facts and by realizations,
> with your heart and mind,
> when you're a faithful speaker.

2

Sometimes I think "Wow! I am doing great. I am really leading
an intelligent discussion. No one here knows as much as I." And
sometimes, "They don't seem interested. Why don't I study more?"

Holding my nonsense ideas at a distance, I proceed mainstream
to *siddhānta*. Glancing at the clock . . . Strive for an objective presen-
tation. Step back from the moment and see where the class is going,
now redirect it, call on that person whose hand was raised minutes
ago. Feel regret for that poor example you just spoke—try to make
up for it, don't get dry, but neither opinionated. Swim through
the fifty-minute period discussing the *guru* in *Caitanya-
caritāmṛta*. . . .

3

I don't know everything, I pray not to think so. But here is
what the *śāstra* says. Are my own comments shallow? Who is *śikṣā*?
Who is *dīkṣā*? Don't speak your "I think."

4

Bhaktisiddhānta dāsa asked how we may preach to the
brījābāsīs who say that Kṛṣṇa is their *guru*. He said one man told
him that when he performs *yajñas* in his home Nārada and Brahmā
attend. So they don't feel the need to join us. We agreed that when
we devotees become more advanced then we will be able to attract
even *brījābāsīs* to pure Kṛṣṇa consciousness.

Caitanyadeva dāsa then said in Vṛndāvana every tree is a *kalpa-
vṛkṣa* (wish-fulfilling tree), so why shouldn't sincere prayers for

pure devotional service be answered? I replied that there is no reason that they will not be answered.

5

It is difficult to hear another man speak for long. The tuning apparatus strays off and on. Why is it? Do you think he cannot speak as well as you? Do you think they pay more attention when you speak? After all, it is *Śrīmad-Bhāgavatam*—we all need it; let's drop the competition as to "Who is the best speaker?" There is gold in there.

But I heard this before. Doesn't he know we covered this same subject last week? (How Mahārāja Parīkṣit did not accept Śukadeva Gosvāmī's teaching on atonement.) Yes, but why shouldn't I listen to the purport?

During the class, sparrows flit around the lecture hall, and the small *gurukula* boys drift off into mental space, while a hundred adult devotees try to hear *Śrīmad-Bhāgavatam*.

About the time of death, the speaker says, "We must spend more time hearing and chanting, and less time in eating and sleeping." He may not be a perfect speaker or devotee, but nothing he says should be rejected. Now he tells a story of a devotee who drove a car off the road at high speed and called out, "Hare Kṛṣṇa!" You chant out of fear at first, he says, but as you develop your Kṛṣṇa consciousness you become fearless and you step on the head of death.

6

The devotee giving the *Śrīmad-Bhāgavatam* class was one I usually cannot pay attention to. But I was determined this time to hear *Śrīmad-Bhāgavatam* from him, instead of disliking his face, or his grammatical idiosyncrasies—such as his sticking the word *that* in the beginning of sentences where it doesn't belong. He is a good scholar, and so I acted as the swan who removes milk from the water. By dividing the distraction from the essence, I tasted the milk of *Śrīmad-Bhāgavatam* for my eternal benefit.

He said, "That this body is like a dream for the soul." We really have nothing to do with the body in the material world. We come here and act as the lords but actually we are simple, loving servants of Kṛṣṇa. Real life is to love Kṛṣṇa and live with Him in Vṛndāvana.

91

Vṛndāvana: Signs of Spring

"Of seasons
I am
flower-bearing spring."

1

Why can't I just *be*
in Kṛṣṇa's abode,
like the *brījābāsīs*?
Why am I so absorbed
in my own ups and downs?

If I can't let go,
at least let me be guided
by Vaiṣṇava behavior,
and in the meantime
I can hear the mourning dove.

2

Spring in Braja means
the *janiya* are in bloom,
pūjārīs use
sandalwood paste on the foreheads
of Śrī Kṛṣṇa and His devotees.

Nīm trees have new sprouts,
spinach in the market place,
the Yamunā not so chill,
and in the room below me
Godbrothers argue
about the role of the *guru* in ISKCON.

The peacocks
show full plumes.

Departures

1

Mail from the U.S.A. A temple president writes that he is in desperate financial condition, but he hopes that I am savoring the mellow of Vṛndāvana. Why should I be savoring when others are struggling to maintain? "I will end this letter," a friend writes, "because I do not wish to break your Vṛndāvana *bhajana* and meditation." But another advises, "When there is a fire, even a scholar may pick up a bucket."

2

A man walking across the Ramaṇa-reti field is carrying a staff with a piece of saffron tied to the end. Vāruṇa asks him the significance of the rod. He says it is in honor of Vasant Panchami (fifth day of March). Everything is blooming, flowers are yellow and orange, so he is celebrating like that. He said Vasant Panchami also has a relation to Kṛṣṇa *līlā*, but he doesn't know what it means.

To me, Vasant Panchami means that I can stay only a few more days in Vṛndāvana. How is it that this Braja fellow is so carefree that he carries a pole declaring spring? I admire his easy way as he walks through the dust. But I am also glad to be myself. Let us be who we are, and help one another to remember Kṛṣṇa.

ACKNOWLEDGEMENTS

Production — Vidura dāsa, Ṭhākura Haridāsa dāsa
Design — Yamarāja dāsa
Artwork — Jagannātha-devī dāsī, Gopīnātha-devī dāsī, Vṛndāvana
    Cooperative Trust
Layout — Madanamohana dāsa
Proofreading — Prāṇadā-devī dāsī
Typesetting — Subha-lakṣmī-devī dāsī
Cover Illustration—Līlā Avatāra-devī dāsī